Sitting Buddha

Zen Meditation for Everyone

Daishin Morgan

Throssel Hole Press • United Kingdom

Published by:

Throssel Hole Press
Throssel Hole Buddhist Abbey
Carrshield, Hexham
Northumberland NE47 8AL • United Kingdom
Tel: +44 (0, 1434 345204
email: gd@throssel.org.uk
Website: www.throssel.org.uk

Copyright © Daishin Morgan, 2004
Edited and designed by Rev. Oriana LaChance
Illustrations by Rev. Gareth Milliken

Printed by Tyneside Free Press, Newcastle, UK
Please seek permission before reproducing.

ISBN: 0-9549139-0-6

Contents

CHAPTER I

Zazen and Buddhist Practice

"Zazen is about coming to realize what you have had from the beginning, rather than seeking some experience that will give you fulfilment and solve all your problems."

"SITTING BUDDHA" is about zazen, a term that literally means "sitting meditation", but has come to be used for a very particular and fundamental meditation that is the root practice of Sōtō Zen Buddhism, the school that includes the Serene Reflection Meditation tradition transmitted by Rev. Master Jiyu-Kennett. In helping to bring this tradition to the West, Rev. Master Jiyu often used the traditional Chinese term "serene reflection meditation" as a descriptive name and I use that interchangeably with the term zazen.

First of all, it is helpful to place serene reflection meditation into its Buddhist context. The Buddha's teaching was focussed on the one purpose of showing how to find the end of suffering. He identified the cause of suffering as the afflictions of ignorance and desire and set out a path leading to liberation from these afflictions. That path begins with the recognition of the need to train oneself. This arises from an inner prompting and an observation of how suffering touches everyone, that all things are impermanent and there is nothing substantial in which we can find true refuge. Next comes the need for an ethical life for ourselves so that we can know peace and tranquillity, and to help others, since through sympathetic understanding we realize that others suffer in the same way as we do.

The desire to help all beings and develop the mind of compassion is fundamental to the path of training in Buddhism. Once we begin to practise, our experience gradually gives rise to wisdom which is the essential counterpart of compassion. The way unfolds like a spiral: as we sort out our lives and develop a little wisdom, we are able to see more clearly; this reveals the need to train more deeply which gives rise to greater compassion and again deepens our wisdom—and so it goes on until enlightenment is realized. Exhortations to lead a good life have no value without the means to develop insight into suffering and the nature of our lives so that we can see how to change. Serene reflection meditation gives us that means.

The Buddha taught that suffering is caused by misreading our senses and interpreting the data in a manner that suggests an "I". It seems as though stuff happens to "me". I have the impression of being one thing and the world around me another thing. I am drawn to seek pleasure and avoid pain. This basic motivation has its roots in the feeling of an "I" set against the world. This "I" is very insecure and wants lots of reassurance. It finds wealth reassuring, love reassuring—anything that bolsters it, the

"I" wants, even craves. The "I" is acutely aware of its vulnerability and is repelled by whatever it sees as a threat. Anger arises when the "I" is thwarted or threatened. This anger ranges from the mildest irritation to a rage in which we wish to completely destroy others. All manner of delusive states of mind, like jealousy and pride, have their origin in this "I".

In questioning the basic assumption that this "I" is real and permanent, Buddhism teaches that the "I" we treasure has no independent existence of its own and cannot exist without everything else being the way that it is. All of existence is interdependent so to view the "I" as a separate thing is an illusion. One can see this quite easily by observing how a small change in the environment also changes how one feels—if the sun comes out my mood brightens, or if I receive some mild criticism it darkens. This "I" of ours is very dependent on the external conditions of life, most of which we cannot control. The more attachment there is to the "I", the more we suffer and the more we are slaves to our greed and fear. The more we suffer the more we seek pleasure or reassurance, yet seeking these things only continues the round of suffering, rather than bringing it to an end. All the things I seek are impermanent and so is my mind. I may get what I want but quite soon I seem to need something else. Thus I get caught in craving and am never satisfied.

Recent research on how craving manifests in the brain has shown that there are two circuits involved, one associated with liking/enjoyment and the other with wanting. "Often these two go together, so we want things that we like. But in craving, the circuitry associated with wanting appears to be strengthened and the circuitry associated with liking appears to be weakened. Because our sense of liking or enjoyment declines and our wanting increases, we want more and more and we like less and less. We just keep wanting—but we need more to enjoy it as much. This is a major problem that underlies craving."[1]

Buddhism has developed highly subtle meditation methods for dealing with craving, as well as anger and the various states of delusion. Dōgen's teaching on zazen is one of the fullest developments of this rich heritage. As one goes into it more and more deeply, greed, hatred and delusion begin to fall away. As they do so, one discovers how to live from the compassion, love and wisdom that are uncovered within oneself.

The monk who brought Sōtō Zen to Japan from China was Great Master Dōgen (1200–1253). He taught that zazen is an expression of Buddhahood and that to sit in zazen is to manifest Buddha Nature or enlightenment. We are the Buddha Nature since all of existence is inseparable from it. To sit in zazen is to let go of our involvement with greed, anger and delusion so that Buddha Nature can shine of itself. From this perspective, zazen is not a method for realizing enlightenment; it is enlightenment itself. However, when one is unfamiliar with this territory, one needs a little practical help to get started.

Zazen is the most fundamental level of awareness within the mind. It is a pure knowing that in itself is bright and complete. It is the primordial mind that everyone has and is our true nature, but it takes a lot of practice to be able to recognize it and then to actualize it in life. Once knowledge of the true nature begins to be awakened within you, there is a light that—even through all the turmoil of life and training—never goes out completely, provided you have a deep commitment to continue your training. The residue of the passions will still arise, and it becomes

[1]Quoted in *Destructive Emotions and How We Can Overcome Them, a Dialogue with the Dalai Lama,* narrated by Daniel Goleman, Bloomsbury 2003.

even more important to work on them, but the path remains clear, if you keep going. The knowledge of the true nature underlies whatever comes and goes. Although one may grieve or experience all kinds of misfortune, beneath it is an undiminished bright knowing that the universe is pure just as it is. One can only come to this place if one is willing to let go of everything that the mind attaches to. If you give rise to clinging, then you will obscure it once more. If you recognize and relinquish that mistake, you find you never left this place. If you are unwilling to let go of the ego and its attachments, then you cannot know the true nature. To come to it we have to sit with a keen and clear mind that is not deliberately giving rise to thoughts and feelings, yet is aware of whatever thoughts or feelings may come. We have to adopt the nature of this pure mind in order to know it, and this is ultimately possible because we are that mind. Rev. Master Jiyu put this in a nutshell: "Look with the eye of a Buddha and you will see the heart of a Buddha."

Once you know the true nature and begin to live from it, a confidence and joy manifests naturally. Most important of all, there is a deep abiding concern for others and the basis of your life becomes what is good to do, rather than what "I" want. Buddhism teaches that to utterly trust the true nature leads to Buddhahood itself where greed, hatred and delusion finally come to a permanent end.

In my experience the true nature is realized gradually. As the form this takes can be quite varied, one should not expect the sudden flash of understanding so emphasized in some zen literature. I have found it best not to emphasize *kenshō,* often defined as seeing the true nature in a moment of experience, in teaching zazen. To use the experience of kenshō as a carrot to tempt the donkey of the will into practising is counterproductive. It is not helpful to strive for particular experiences. Training for everyone involves giving up clinging to all forms, ideas and objects of desire. When we grasp at any thing, our path will be blocked. Also, if great emphasis is placed upon kenshō, the result can lead to a sense of unworthiness in the sincere heart for whom training does not necessarily unfold in that way. The experience of enlightenment is not subject to our bidding. Many of those who practise long-term and with great sincerity do not experience kenshō as a sudden flash of awakening but as a deep inner change that happens over time. This may be so gradual that one is not even aware of it at the time it is taking place. But then, quite without drama, one realizes what has been there from the beginning. For others, a sudden experience plays a significant role in this process and a lot of what has been written about zen is from their perspective.

Zazen is about coming to realize what you have had from the beginning, rather than seeking some experience that will give you fulfilment and solve all your problems. Accepting what comes and developing the willingness to see oneself clearly are the necessary keys. Rather than living to get what we want, zazen transforms us into people who are grateful for whatever we have and thereby we become experts at finding jewels in the most surprising places.

CHAPTER 2

The Physical Aspects of Zazen

*"By grounding yourself physically in the body
you have a good basis for zazen,
as mind and body are inseparable."*

THERE ARE FOUR positions for meditation described in the Buddhist sūtras—standing, sitting, walking and lying down. Wherever you are, whatever the circumstances, you can always do zazen, even if you are ill or dying. These recommended positions refer to the formal practice and learning them helps to facilitate the right attitude of mind, as well as deepen one's mindful awareness of the body. The sitting position is the primary one for formal practice but no matter which position you are in, it is essential to be grounded and focussed within your physical body. When Buddhists meet each other and wish to express respect, we put our palms together with the fingers pointing upwards in a gesture called the *gasshō*. As well as engendering respect and gratitude, it is an expressive way of bringing yourself together. Mind and body are one, so being aware of your body gives you a basis for understanding the mind; it provides a starting point and a place of stability to which you can always return. If you are settled and grounded within your body, then your mind will have some stability too. If the mind is just trying to understand itself without reference to the body, it can spin off into abstraction and unreality thus becoming divorced from the here and now.

The Standing Position

Although sitting is the primary posture for meditation, I have found the standing position to be the easiest one in which to learn what it means to be present within the body in a way that is relaxed and centred. You can try this by standing up straight with your heels about two fists apart and with your arms hanging loosely by your sides, while letting your shoulders and abdomen relax. Have your knees slightly bent, just enough so that they are not locked. Now feel the weight of your head being carried by your neck and shoulders and let them relax. In your mind, follow the weight down your body. Feel the weight passing down your arms, through your wrists and out through your fingers, relaxing you as it goes. Relax your shoulders and feel the weight of your torso resting on your pelvis; relax your buttocks and pelvis so your weight goes down your thighs and on through your knees and calves to your feet and then on into the floor. Feel how the floor absorbs your weight so that you and the floor are one. Stand there for a while like this with your attention focussed just on your physical presence.

When standing formally in meditation, as is done during a temple ceremony or for walking meditation, place your left hand with the thumb gently held within a fist at the level of the base of your sternum with the right hand covering it. The forearms should be level and parallel with the floor. This hand position is known as *shashu*. When you move your arms into this position, keep your shoulders relaxed. This may be hard at first, as the tendency is to stand rather stiffly, but as you become aware of tensions keep letting them go. As you relax, other muscles take over and your weight is held evenly by all of you. The body has a natural source of energy that will hold you once you learn to trust it. All the formal meditation positions have some aspect that requires a degree of muscle tone to maintain. Learning to maintain this tone is connected with remaining present in your body and is extremely helpful. It takes time to learn how to do it in a relaxed way. The position described here is also the basis used for walking meditation, but more on that later.

Whenever you are standing, say waiting in a queue, you can take this position and be very grounded and centred (without the formal hand position which might feel a bit odd in the middle of an airport). This is

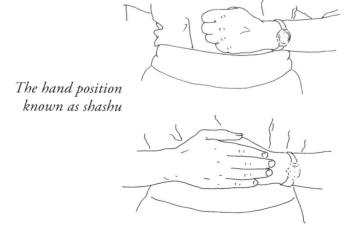

The hand position known as shashu

The left thumb is held gently within the fist. Then the right hand is placed over it.

extremely helpful in dealing with stress, worry and a host of other emotions and tensions. All the positions for meditation can be adapted to suit the situation you are in, once you get the idea of how they work.

Sitting Meditation

This is the best posture of all for meditation and its most important feature is to have your back in the right position. To get an idea of the correct position, take the standing position described above only this time place your forearms in the small of your back. Feel around and notice how your back is, notice the degree of the lumbar curve in the small of your back when you stand straight. This is how it should feel when you are sitting.

Using a Chair

I will begin with how to do zazen on a chair, as this position is one nearly everyone can manage right away without unnecessary discomfort. Whatever sitting position we adopt, the whole architecture of the zazen posture depends upon the "sitting bones" which are the lowest part of the pelvis. You can feel these knobbly bones when you sit on your hands. To sit up straight without strain, these sitting bones need to be supported in such a way that the pelvis is tipped slightly forward. This in turn allows the lower back to assume a slight inward curve in the lumbar region and the upper body can then be comfortably supported with the shoulders relaxed and the chest open.

Sit on an upright chair with a flat seat or on something like a piano stool. It is important to avoid chairs that have a backward slope to the seat. Position your sitting bones in the middle of the seat; if the chair has a back, don't lean against it but sit up straight. Place your heels about two

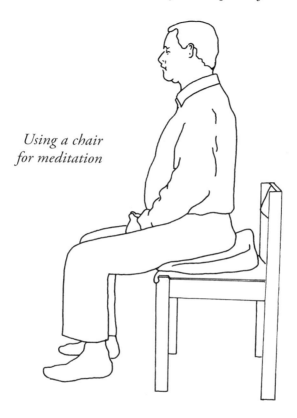

*Using a chair
for meditation*

fists apart and make sure your feet are flat on the floor and more or less parallel with each other. Position your feet far enough forward so that your shins are approximately vertical; let your knees be apart as feels natural. To check that your back is in the right position, put your forearms in the small of your back again. Your back should feel like it did when you were standing.

It will be important to have a chair that is the right height for you. If you look at the illustration, you can see the model's thighs are sloping slightly downward. You may need to add a cushion if the chair is too low, or place something under your feet if the chair is too high. It is worth taking a bit of time to get this right. Once you have done that, sit on your hands and feel the sitting bones. Take a moment to feel the curve of bone that rests against your fingers, then slump down so that your pelvis rotates back and you have a stooped posture. Then sit up straight again and, as you do so, feel how the sitting bones pivot. Do this a few times feeling the bones rotate slightly as your pelvis moves back and forth. To get the support you need in meditation, the sitting bones need to be supported on the forward edge of their curve so that your pelvis is tipped forward slightly

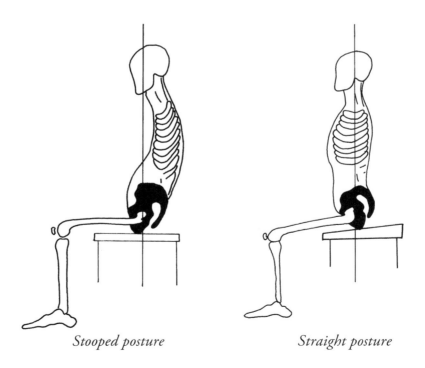

Stooped posture   *Straight posture*

and your back takes the right lumbar curve without having to strain to hold it all in place.

You may find that having a wedge-shaped cushion to sit on helps to achieve this forward curve. Alternatively, you can fold a towel or flat cushion to achieve the same effect as the wedge. An important point to watch is not to force your lumbar area to curve inwards too much. If the chair is too high for you and your thighs slope down too steeply, this may tend to happen. If in doubt about the correct lumbar curve, stand up again and check how the curve should be in the way described above.

The abdomen should be allowed to relax; don't hold yourself in. Everyone experiences tension at times in meditation and this is often felt in the abdomen. Don't worry if it feels tense. The important thing is not to fight but to accept the presence of the tension and it will begin to relax in time.

You can find the right position for your head by imagining a string attached to the crown of your head. If the string were pulled gently upwards, your neck would lengthen and your chin would tuck in just slightly and this is what you want to achieve. The head should rest on your neck and shoulders in a relaxed way and feel weightless, *i.e.* there should be no strain in holding it there. Keep your eyes open and lower your gaze to about 45 degrees from the horizontal. If you normally wear glasses, it is best to keep them on. Your eyes should be in focus; however, do not pick out a point on the floor or wall in front of you and stare at it. Do not concern yourself with what you see—your attention needs to be inward. Keeping your eyes open helps to keep you grounded here, where you are, and is one means of countering dreamy states of mind that sap your energy. Place your tongue against the back of your top teeth and keep your lips closed. The teeth should be just closed, not clamped shut. Breathe normally through your nose.

Place your hands in your lap so your arms are relaxed. If you find it difficult to relax your arms, a small cushion or other soft item placed under your hands may help. Place your hands as shown below with the thumbs lightly touching—so that you could just hold a piece of paper between them without letting it fall. Don't press your thumbs together. This hand posture requires the maintenance of some muscle tone to keep your thumbs in place, in the same way that the pelvis and the back do. When people fall asleep or get drowsy in meditation, their thumbs usually droop.

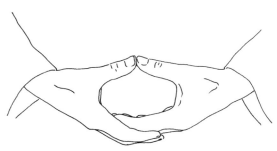

The hand position

It is important not to lean off to one side, or backwards or forwards. To settle yourself into the right position, it helps to sway the body in a circular motion, gradually decreasing the size of the circles, until you have centred yourself. The idea is to sense from the inside what being centred feels like. Having done this, you should then sit steadily, letting go of thoughts as they arise by keeping your attention focussed on your physical presence.

Using Cross-Legged Postures

For those who are able, the traditional postures of cross-legged sitting are recommended, but they are not essential. For sitting in this way you will need a *zafu* or round meditation cushion, although you can improvise with a folded blanket. The height of the cushion will depend upon your physical shape so it is worth experimenting. Your sitting bones should be on the edge of the zafu. Don't sit too far back or you will cut

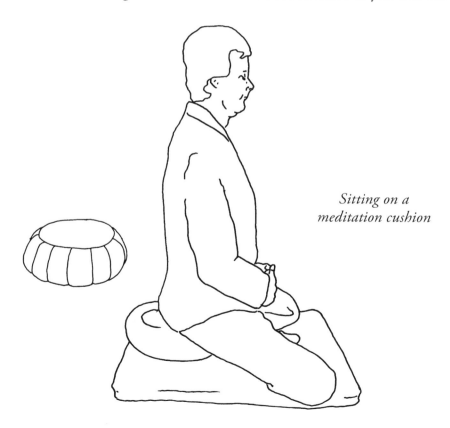

*Sitting on a
meditation cushion*

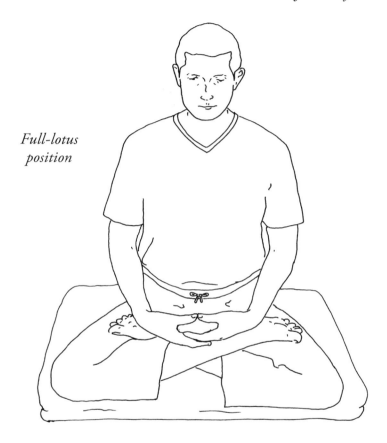

Full-lotus position

the circulation in your legs. The zafu will slope forward providing the necessary pelvic tilt and thus the correct lumbar curve.

The lotus position, where the right foot is placed upon the left thigh and the left foot is placed upon the right thigh, is recommended by Dōgen in his zazen instructions, along with the half-lotus position where just one foot is placed upon the opposite thigh.

*Half-lotus
position*

A further variant is called the Burmese position (see the following page) where both feet remain on the floor. Whatever cross-legged position you use, both knees must be on the floor or your sitting will be very unstable. To begin with, try sitting in one of these positions for a few minutes at a time and gradually increase the length of time as your body adapts. Don't strain and overdo it or you will cause damage to your knees. When

Burmese position

using any of the cross-legged postures, it is a good idea to vary which foot you have to the front or on top, otherwise you can develop a twist to your pelvis and spine after some years of always sitting the same way.

Cross-legged sitting is quite difficult for many Westerners, some of whom have differently proportioned bodies to most Asian people. Also, if you have not accustomed yourself to sitting in this way when young, it can be more difficult to adapt in later life. When sitting for long periods you can damage yourself, so do take care. However, if you are able to sit in this way, and a good number of Westerners can do so, then it is the recommended position.

Using a Bench

The use of a meditation bench is a very good alternative. A meditation bench is used in a kneeling position. It should be as low as possible so that the underside of the seat just clears your upturned heels. Larger people may

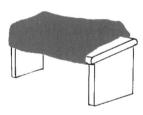

Sitting on a bench with the hands resting on a small cushion

find this position creates painful pressure behind their knees. This can be helped by increasing the height of the bench, but if the space between the front of the seat and the floor is greater than about 6 inches, the pelvis will be pushed too far forward making the lumbar curve too great and this can cause damage. In this case, a chair is a better option. Note that there is a forward tilt to the seat of the bench to help your pelvis take the right position. This forward tilt should not be more than about 10 degrees from the horizontal or it will strain the lower back.

These days I have to do zazen sitting on a chair and I can attest to the fact that it works perfectly well. The other positions do assist in giving a sense of groundedness, which is why they are recommended, but one can be well-grounded on a chair. Zazen is not meant to be an endurance test. You will need to develop your will as you sit, in order to overcome distractions and to look at those aspects of yourself that you may tend to shy away from, but there is no need to add to the difficulty by being unnecessarily ascetic.

Grounding Yourself

The physical posture of zazen is the foundation of meditation. By grounding yourself physically in the body you have a good basis for zazen, as mind and body are inseparable. As you sit, let yourself be conscious of your weight just as you did with the standing exercise described above. Letting your body relax, feel how your head rests on your neck and shoulders, how your spine is supported by your pelvis, the sitting bones and the cushion; feel your weight travelling down your body and into the chair and into the ground through your feet or knees. Your whole body is being supported or held by the earth and there is no need to draw a distinction between you and the ground. Now you are sitting like a mountain! Grounding yourself like this is the foundation you can come back to whenever you find yourself getting lost or distracted. Zazen is to completely do the one thing you are doing without letting yourself be carried away by *thinking* about what you are doing. Sitting is about as simple as it gets, yet we are complicated creatures and so there is more to learn about the nature of the mind. Before we get into that, I will describe how to do walking meditation and meditation when lying down.

Walking Meditation or *Kinhin*

When we do more than one period of meditation, we do *kinhin,* or walking meditation, between periods of sitting. The sitting period can be any length up to about forty minutes and walking meditation is done usually for about ten minutes. When the sitting period ends, don't move suddenly, but sway gently from side to side and then slowly stand up. Stand in the formal standing posture described above and begin to walk slowly, taking steps about the length of your foot. Keep your eyes open and lowered as you did when sitting. If your mind wanders, come back to your body again. The pace should be no slower than one small step per breath. Sometimes the pace may be increased to help counteract the tendency to become foggy-minded and lethargic. When doing walking meditation with others, everyone forms a circle and begins to move together. There is no signal to start; just keep pace with the person in front without allowing the gap between you to lengthen. In this way everyone moves as one. You will find that when you visit a temple, there is some emphasis placed on doing things in a particular way and

Walking meditation

in tune with everyone else. This is to encourage an interdependent way of being that is aware of others and cultivates a willingness to act in concert with them.

Meditation Lying Down

One should only meditate lying down when you are ill and unable to meditate sitting up in the usual way. It is important not to be lazy. However, many people have bad backs or other physical problems from time to time that allow no alternative. It is also useful to know how to meditate

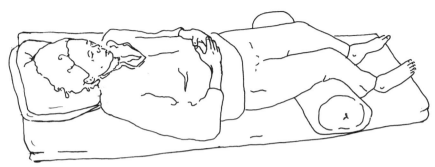

Meditation lying on your back

for a few minutes in bed at night before going to sleep. There are two positions that can be used: on your back with the knees raised or supported; and lying on your right side.

In the meditation hall at Throssel, we recommend using the method of lying on your back, sometimes rather unattractively called corpse pose. It helps to have a rolled blanket or other soft item to place under your knees. Keep your feet about three or four fists apart. Most back problems are helped by being supported in this way. I find that the best hand position is to bring your hands together over your lower abdomen with the thumbs touching so you form a variation of the oval shape used when you are sitting. An alternative is to put your hands in shashu as described for formal standing meditation; you may find you need a cushion under each elbow to allow your hands to meet and your arms to relax.

The alternative posture is to lie on your right side with your knees drawn about halfway up (see the following page). Support your head with your right hand so that your palm is against your cheek and your thumb is positioned just behind your ear lobe. Your left hand is placed on the top

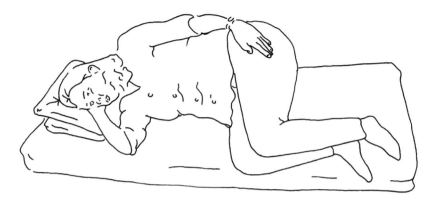

Meditation in the parinirvana position

of your left hip. This is the classic pose said to have been adopted by the Buddha at the time of his death or parinirvana. It is an excellent posture for meditating in bed just before sleep.

The positions described above are those used for what we call formal meditation or zazen. However, zazen can be done in any position; those described above are the most helpful for formal practice, but we don't do formal practice all the time. It is good to meditate quietly in an armchair or while strolling along a country lane or while doing the shopping. To really get to the heart of meditation, it has to gradually become the "default position" of the mind. This takes practice and to come to it you need to practise zazen no matter what you are doing. The essence of it is to come back to what you are doing here and now and do it with all of your being.

Although I have covered the main points, everyone is a little different and these instructions may need to be adapted to suit the individual. I recommend seeking instruction from a qualified teacher when you can, rather than relying on these written instructions alone.

CHAPTER 3

The Mind
of Meditation

"To meditate is to do nothing:
you don't need to express anything,
ask for anything or reject anything."

WHEN DOING ZAZEN we are giving expression to our true nature, by that I mean our actual existence in the present moment. The past has already gone and the future has not yet come—so where are we? You cannot answer that question by thinking about it, because as soon as you formulate an idea of where you are, you have already moved on. The answer lies in just being—or "just sitting" as zazen is sometimes called. This involves using the mind in a new way. To do that you have to let go of thoughts and feelings as they arise or else you will be concerned with the thought or feeling of the last moment and not really be present. You are not meditating if you sit there thinking about what you did yesterday or what you will do in a moment or two. It is no good trying to prevent

thoughts from arising; they occur because you have a normally function-
ing mind. Yet you don't have to follow those thoughts; you can simply
let go of them. A thought that spontaneously arises is just a thought. It
is not right or wrong, but what you do with it is very important. If an
old resentment comes to mind and you let it go, anger becomes less. If,
on the other hand, you indulge the thought by letting it run on and on,
then hatred is nurtured. What is important is to come to the right relationship with your thoughts: not holding on to them and not pushing
them away.

The first thing is to begin to discern the role of the will in thinking.
For example, a memory seems to spring from nowhere of something that
happened on your last holiday—that is a spontaneous thought. Now you
start to think about where you will go for your holiday this year—that is a
deliberate thought. It is this deliberate thought that you have to set aside.
Don't worry about the spontaneous thoughts, although as your practice
deepens you will find more thoughts are deliberate than at first seemed
to be the case. Learning how to regain control of your deliberate thinking is crucial. Otherwise, you are the slave of thinking and can never be
internally still. To know your own presence and "just sit", you have to
use the pristine mind that is your true nature with nothing volitional
added. Don't try to make the true nature be what you want it to be—let
it alone so you can know the essence of yourself as it is. We are so used to
asserting ourselves, to instantly responding to every thought and feeling
with another thought. We almost never spend time with pure being, just
sitting without asserting the "I". To meditate is to do nothing: you don't
need to express anything, ask for anything or reject anything. The work of
meditation is to free yourself from doing all of these things and to release

yourself from a whole load of mental investments and projections at the same time.

Those thoughts that are not volitional, at least at our current level of awareness, have relatively little effect and so do not disturb zazen, but volitional thoughts keep the mind operating at the level of the phantom "I" discussed in chapter one. When we deliberately think, we create karmic consequence. In other words, we pattern our mind and brains according to how we think and that disposes us to act in similar ways in the future. An idle fantasy may not do anyone else any harm, but it disposes you to more idle fantasy in the future and you then spend much of your life only half present. Most people have the false impression that they cannot control their deliberate thought processes; they try to let them go but the thoughts seem to have a life of their own. You are the one who is thinking your thoughts—nobody else is doing it—and thoughts are dependent upon your will. The difficulty in letting go of thoughts usually arises because we are attached to them; we believe we enjoy thinking them or find them reassuring.

Quite often during meditation people attempt to justify themselves. A memory comes to mind that is a little uncomfortable and they elaborate a whole case for their defence including a rousing speech to the jury. Sometimes we are afraid and thinking is a way of seeking reassurance. Sometimes we just have a dull mind and sit like a pudding. Our thinking may be rational and ordered, but more likely it is a jumble of fantasies, inner dialogues and memories all flitting here and there without much focus.

It is alarming and humbling to see for the first time just how our minds behave. There is an endless variety of answers to why we find sitting in meditation difficult. I find it helpful to notice how many thoughts involve fear or desire somewhere in their motivation. These two are the basic driving forces behind the phantom "I". At this point, it is important to stress that not all these mental activities should be seen as wrong, though they are inappropriate when practising zazen. The ability to think things through is vital to our well being, but if that faculty can never stop, if we are the slave of our thinking rather than its master, then we have a problem.

If I am due to fly somewhere next week, I may find myself having a fantasy about terrorists taking over the aeroplane and me very heroically fighting them off! Said like that it is easy to see the comic side, but I am actually a bit nervous about flying and the mind throws up this reassuring fantasy. To set these thoughts aside, I need to see that I am a bit afraid and willingly sit within the fear. When there is fear, just be frightened and accept it. This is another way of saying look directly at the fear and it loses its power. If I wish to know the true nature, I must be willing to be with things as they are. The remarkable thing is that when I do that, I become free of the affliction. Mental states like fear and desire, as well as other feelings and emotions, are deeply linked to thoughts. In fact, thoughts and emotions are really part of one continuum.

The process is the same when anger arises. It is accompanied by thoughts, usually a rehashing of the events that made me angry or a speculation about what I will do about the situation. Now it is important to watch anger very closely whenever you have the chance to study it through your own direct observation, but don't cultivate it just to see it! When it has arisen, notice what it feels like, notice how it waxes and wanes according to how your thoughts run. It may fade somewhat until you think again of the offence you feel you suffered and off you go again. When this kind of thing happens, we are feeding the anger with the energy of our thoughts. To do zazen is to notice that the anger has arisen; don't get involved in judging it as good or bad, justified or unjustified. Put aside the recurring patterns of thought and you find that perhaps there is a lot of hurt and sadness beneath the anger. There will be thoughts associated with those feelings too; let them go as well and the feelings of hurt will also dissolve. In an instant one can pick up the anger again—in which case repeat the process. If we practise this, in time we become a much less angry person and are able to let anger pass more quickly when it does arise. It is possible to see anger coming and choose not to indulge it. The most obvious way one can see this is through being aware of a rising situation that we know can produce anger and being ready, and most importantly *willing,* to not choose it. If one keeps going with the practice, eventually one can let go of the very cause of the anger—which is the frightened self.

When I was a teenager I quickly grew to my present six foot three inches. My parents and I moved to an old country cottage with low door lintels. My father was also tall and, like me, would bang his head when not being very aware. He would vent his feelings by thumping the lintel with his fist and swearing—a strategy I quickly adopted. When I learned to meditate, I realized it was possible to bang my head and not thump the lintel and swear; even though reeling from the impact, it was possible to remain still inside. There was a moment of choice. The lintel had not meant to do me harm and the frustration was my own feeling of foolishness. I realized I felt sillier thumping the lintel and I could save myself the inner turmoil of the anger.

Other situations where anger arises can be much harder to see coming and often we only realize we are angry after we are already well into it. Even so, with practise we can let go of the thoughts and just contemplate the feeling of anger. If we can do that, the anger will vanish. There is an important point here: we should not direct our effort to making the anger go away. Just don't go on feeding the anger with angry thoughts. We need to accept whatever arises within zazen and be willing to be still with it—don't feed it and don't push it away.

Now why is it that thoughts/emotions disappear when you look directly at them? In Buddhism, memories, thoughts and feelings are all regarded as mental objects. The brain is viewed as a sense organ that is used to perceive mental "things". (There are six senses in Buddhism, the normal five plus the mental sense.) Within our field of mental view, we can only be aware of one thing at a time. We can shift from one mental object to another in less than a blink of an eye; nevertheless, it is only one thing at a time. This means that if our attention is moved away from sustaining the thought stream, then that stream will cease. Anger, desire and fear all depend upon a thought stream for their continued existence; once you are looking directly at them, you cannot continue the thought stream and so they cease. We can get caught up with thoughts again in an instant, but we have a choice whether to invest in them again or not. Much will depend on how willing we are to let them go.

We all know what it is like to lie in bed at night and worry—the useless going round and round the same circle in our minds, rehashing the same "what ifs" but unable to lay the matter to rest. I find it helps to break the stream of thought and give myself a pause in which to redirect my mind. One way I have found to do this is to recite a short scripture or perhaps to recite the Three Refuges: "I take refuge in the Buddha, I take refuge in the Dharma, I take refuge in the Sangha." (One could recite anything here that expresses something of one's true intent in life.) The effect is to break the self-perpetuating thought pattern and to affirm my intention to base my life on what is true rather than on the fantasies and projections that give rise to worry. I need to give expression to these wishes in the manner of my recitation and not just mouth the words. This works if I put my faith in zazen rather than in worrying.

The world we experience is the world created within our own minds. Our thoughts and feelings depend upon how we view the world; they are not absolutes nor are they as solid or as real as they seem. By learning not to be driven by thoughts and feelings, we can see how they are like a fantasy or a dream. Knowing this, we can return to the primordial mind of zazen. Thoughts and feelings do not necessarily stop, but we no longer mistake them for our true nature.

Zazen is about learning to free oneself from the grip of afflictive thoughts, emotions and feelings because they drive us to act in ways we later regret, or they colour the world so that we see our projections rather than reality. This is a serious problem and the source of much suffering and evil. When fearful thoughts are allowed to run on, particularly when they are thoughts about another group, they lead to anger, then to hatred and rage and, under the influence of that, genocide is possible. By doing something about our own thoughts, we are directly reducing the amount and spread of evil in the world. In Buddhism, afflictive mental states are seen as any movement of the mind that tends to obscure the true nature of ourselves and the world. We all have our theories on what needs to be done to make the world a better place—and they almost always concern what other people should do. To undertake the great project of training ourselves in zazen, is to realize that it begins with ourselves.

I have given a rather rough analysis of how the mind gets caught up in its mental objects, be they fantasies, thoughts or emotions. However, in meditation itself one should not analyze at all. In this moment now, "Why?" is not the issue; what matters is that you stop feeding those thoughts. In the same vein, it is important not to judge the thoughts as good or bad, as that just continues the process. Don't judge and don't make excuses, just sit! If you are going to bring the mind under control, you have to do it now—there is no other time. Of course, there are many good and necessary uses of the mind. The whole of the Buddhist sūtras are an example. Zazen needs to become the default position from which we use our abilities to plan, think things through and utilize all the other wonderful abilities we have. You do, however, need the right understanding of what you are doing, the right frame of reference and to know the check points that can prevent you from going too far off the track.

There is one last important piece of advice. When you are meditating, don't sit there watching yourself doing it or you will be trying to split yourself in half. It comes down to trusting that you are meditating unless you see you are not, in which case you also see what you need to drop.

In summary, then, the main points of how to do zazen are to sit up straight and ground yourself in your physical being. Let go of thoughts and emotions as they arise. If you do not feed them, they will cease to disturb you. This leads you closer and closer to your true nature, the primordial mind that is one with reality. Zazen is to just be this mind, which we already are, without adding anything to it. It is to accept all that arises as appearances within the mind. There is no need to fight or judge these appearances; simply let them go by putting aside the thoughts connected to them. Although greed, anger and delusions will continue, we do not have to join in the dance that they invite us to follow. When we sit still in the midst of what comes, we find stability and peace of mind and this is the source of compassion.

CHAPTER 4

Who Is This?

"If we are not our thoughts and feelings,
then what are we? I find this to be a crucial question
that is at the heart of the meaning of zazen."

I HAVE FOUND that one of the first lessons living in a monastery teaches is the need to clearly see the difference between one's feelings and the situation in which they have arisen. It often happens that new monks have difficulty getting on with each other. This is not surprising as monastic life can be very intense, especially as there is no private space and very little opportunity to get away from the pressures. The new monk has to sit in the midst of his or her feelings rather than run away from them. When resentment arises, the monk is taught not to blame the other person but to look directly at their own feelings. It can seem very unjust to be asked to do this, when the other person is patently doing something they should not. Even so, one's first duty is to take responsibility for one's own resentment and not be concerned with what others are doing. This principle is the same in all modes of life.

To be able to separate the two components—the issue that has arisen and your feelings about it—enables you to get your priorities clear. The monk has committed himself or herself to training and this has to come before everything else, despite the natural tendency to get locked in and blame the other person. The issue at stake is always secondary to dealing with an afflicted state of mind. In the heat of the moment, when we feel our personhood has been encroached upon or attacked, that is the very time—indeed the only time—when we can turn resentment around. Then what started as a petty argument can become a truly life-changing moment. This is to bow to the situation. Bowing is the opposite of complaining about how difficult it is. Such sincerity enables a trainee to see what is good to do, because his or her mind is no longer afflicted by resentment.

When sitting in zazen, we have to regard our thoughts and feelings as secondary in importance in the same kind of way. If they are our first concern, then we will go endlessly round and round in circles. A question we have to address is, "Are we our thoughts and feelings?" Clearly, they are a significant component of our experience of life, but to identify with them is a mistake. If we do, then we have no stability but are blown about by every breeze that comes along. For if I feel uncomfortable, then "I" am uncomfortable. That need not be so; one can be quite aware of uncomfortable feelings but remain sitting within the unmoving pure mind of zazen.

If we are not our thoughts and feelings, then what are we? I find this to be a crucial question that is at the heart of the meaning of zazen. When I am having trouble trusting myself to the sitting, I find it helpful to ask, "Who is it that sits?" For this strategy to be part of one's zazen and not simply a technique or method, it is vital to make no move to answer the question other than to look where the question is pointing. It is as if I were to ask you, "What is that behind you?" The only real way to know is to turn round and look for yourself. The question merely serves to bring what is important to your attention. No words, theories or methods are needed other than turning your head. Just so in zazen, "Who is this?" When you look into your heart, any thoughts or feelings are secondary matters that you can leave to take care of themselves.

I experience this as largely a matter of not doing rather than doing. There is nothing to get hold of in response to this question of "Who?" Each seeming level of "me" turns out to be another thought or feeling that passes. I seem to be made up of fleeting thoughts and feelings, some stay for a while, others pass very quickly. That thoughts and feelings arise is not a problem, so long as I do not add my volition to them. What I see is how I interrupt the looking with unnecessary movements of the mind. All my volition needs to be taken up with the act of looking/being. I cannot stand apart from what is seen and name it; I can only be it. I can be the sitting person and that person is sitting Buddha. This involves letting body and mind fall away, that is to let go of all conceptions of myself and the world and just sit. What is left is zazen doing zazen.

Zazen or enlightenment is not about finding a particular state of mind, for all states of mind are fleeting and cannot be relied upon. When you know who is sitting, you know sitting Buddha. This expression is a bit strange; why not say sitting *like* a Buddha? I prefer to say sitting Buddha because there is nobody sitting *like* a Buddha; there is just sitting Buddha. That Buddha never stops sitting, but we must awaken to her presence—not that sitting Buddha is either male or female.

Original Enlightenment

Sitting Buddha is another way of speaking about Buddha Nature or the nature of enlightenment. We usually conceive of living the Buddhist life as a path going from delusion to enlightenment, as is implied by referring to it as the Way. In the Zen tradition, there is another view which stems from the understanding that Buddha Nature is not subject to coming and going; it is not born and does not die. Buddha Nature, therefore, is not something we acquire through training. The spiritual life in zen is realizing Buddha Nature in the present moment. Because all beings are enlightened from the very beginning, this way of understanding Buddha Nature is called original enlightenment. We have nothing missing, we cannot be separate from the truth—realizing this is not so simple. We have to awaken to our original nature, our enlightened nature.

In a very practical way, this means that in the course of our training we need to look at what we have, rather than focussing on what we believe we lack or need to understand. I spent many years in training believing that my purpose was to become one with the Buddha Nature. By doing so, I saw myself as missing something I needed. I was always trying to look ahead of myself, hoping and praying that what I believed I needed would come over the horizon. As I tried to move forward to meet it, I pushed it away in front of me. I have come to see this mode of training as based upon inadequacy. It takes a lot of faith to practise zazen. However, the faith I am talking about is faith in one's true nature, not faith in something outside of yourself. It is to believe that at the heart of your being there is that which is complete—the source of compassion and wisdom. If you can trust your own being, then you are already realizing your true nature. To mistrust it is absurd, and to be caught up in mistaking thoughts, feelings and emotions for the truly indestructible one, the one who experiences all these things, who is this?

CHAPTER 5

The Life of Practice

"Regular zazen seems unspectacular,
yet it gradually gives rise to far-reaching changes."

THE WHOLE WONDERFUL process that Buddhism opens up of releasing our minds from their afflictions is a lifetime's undertaking. It needs to penetrate to all areas of life, including work, family life and leisure. Most people live with a lot of pressure and stress and this can be difficult. It is not so much a matter of balancing all these elements while trying to add in your meditation practice. A more helpful way is to see how the practice is at the heart of all these things and how you can find creative ways of practising within them. And, of course, you will have to make some room because however good you become at the informal aspects of zazen, there is no substitute for formal sitting.

A Daily Routine

It helps to have a regular routine for meditation as a foundation for the day. Monastic life has a lot of routine, partly because it takes a great deal of training to uproot the more persistent difficulties and even to see some of them in the first place. The value of routine is that when it comes time to sit, you just do it without getting into that "shall I, shan't I" business, for excuses usually are not hard to find. You can make habit work for you in this way.

The ideal is to meditate in the morning when you get up and again in the evening. In the normal course of events, once you have become accustomed to zazen, you can sit reasonably easily for half an hour at a time and it is good to aim at that. But I recommend keeping the minimum commitment you make to something you know you can always manage no matter what. So I suggest just making a commitment to sit down in meditation twice a day. If you feel you *have* to sit for half an hour, it is easy to tell yourself you don't have time or you are too tired and sometimes, of course, that will be true. You have no excuse when all you need to do is sit for just a few moments. The hardest bit is sitting down to meditate in the first place. Once you are there you can manage more than you might expect. Gradually build up the time you spend in meditation, rather than setting yourself unrealistic targets.

It helps to have a special place to meditate, a corner of your bedroom or some other quiet place. Having a statue of the Buddha, some flowers, a candle and incense is very helpful. Keep this place clean and tidy, especially the altar, if you choose to have one.

Everyone finds that sometimes the mind shies away from sitting because it is bored or uneasy. These are good times to persist and literally sit through such feelings so they are not in control. One of the rules we have at the monastery is not to fidget during meditation periods. If you need to move to prevent damaging your body, then do so, especially while you are learning a new sitting position. You will not disturb others by quietly moving to another position or drawing your knees up for a while and then resuming your zazen posture. Fidgeting is another matter. It is all those movements driven by a restless mind. We scratch our face, shuffle our feet and sigh or make any number of other small movements, rather than settle to doing zazen. It helps to resolve not to move and then, even if there is an itch, you do not have to scratch it. This is a very important thing. We are subject to so many itches—literal and metaphorical—that learning not to respond to them, to develop the capacity to sit through them, is an essential to freedom. While we *have* to scratch every itch, we are a slave. Instead, we can quietly contemplate the sensation of the itch and it soon passes.

We each have to find creative ways of putting zazen into practice. When people come to the monastery and see all the forms we use, they can make the mistake of thinking they must do it like that when they get home. The forms are here to help us discern the spirit so we can go away and apply that spirit in whatever conditions we meet. We don't need to be stiff about it. Zazen done properly leads to a flexible mind.

Regular zazen seems unspectacular, yet it gradually gives rise to far-reaching changes. Your commitment to practice is a statement of what is important in your life. We can have all manner of ideas, but when it comes to actually transforming your life there is nothing like practising the teaching. If you have a temple near you or a meditation group where you can sit with others, this is really helpful. However you practise, it is important to check in with a qualified teacher from time to time. Even if you feel all is going well, it is still a good idea, as it is so easy to fool oneself or just mistake some of the signposts in training.

Your attempts to practise meditation should not become a war with you fighting for the space and time to meditate. Unselfishness is at the heart of zazen. However, you may need to reflect on how your time is spent. If you are in a relationship, talk to your partner about your desire to meditate. To them it may feel like an act of exclusion, and indeed it may be if you use it in the wrong way. Obviously, if you both are wanting to sit that helps, but beware of trying to convert your partner. If you are finding meditation helpful and life-changing it is natural to want to share it, but the zeal of the new meditator is best directed inwards to keeping the practice going. If it changes you for the better, then that will be the best advertisement. Find a way that is right within your situation.

Meditation in Activity

When sitting, just sit; when working, just work. In other words, keeping your mind with what you are doing is the key. This is often referred to as mindfulness training. It can gradually encompass all your activities. You can only do working meditation if you are prepared to totally do what you are doing. If it is good to do, then it is worth putting your whole being into it; if it is not good to do, then don't do it. This is the key to a full life. However, as in formal meditation, don't try and be aware of yourself being mindful. Notice that if you do that, you are trying to be two people—the one who is working and the one who is watching the worker. I find it is best to assume you are meditating, whatever you are doing, unless you see that you are not, in which case bring yourself back to the job in hand. It is easiest to learn this doing simple things—walking to work, cleaning round the house or weeding the garden. If you get very scattered, it helps to stop for a moment and stand or sit still using the method for grounding yourself described in chapter two. Don't get cross and scold yourself; that only adds to the problem. When you notice that your mind is wandering, you have already come back to yourself. At that moment, the key is to be willing to let go of whatever you are thinking about and be with the job in hand. It is a fallacy to believe that repetitive jobs are made easier by being somewhere else in your mind. All that does is take away your life. You can help yourself enormously by doing only one thing at a time. Turn the radio off when you are reading or eating; when listening to music, give it your whole attention, don't use it as an anaesthetic. Repetitive work is a particularly valuable meditation practice. Although you may have ten things needing doing, you can only ever do one at a time, even if you move between different jobs very quickly.

It helps to guard your senses to some extent. For example, when standing at the checkout in a supermarket, don't let your mind glaze over; keep your attention focussed. You may notice the magazine racks and their headlines—they are deliberately designed to distract you—but you don't have to play the game. It is a very good place to do standing meditation.

Keeping your mind on what you are doing applies to enjoyable activities as much as to anything else. It is good to enjoy things. The life of practice involves dedicating oneself to the good of all beings and we need to remember that we are one of these beings. If we don't take care of ourselves, it is all the harder to keep going. Some time to relax and renew helps to fulfil our purpose. Zazen should increase our ability to enjoy whatever opportunities life presents.

Interacting with others is a vital part of training. It is the place where we can see ourselves in a way that we may never succeed in doing if we only sit in meditation. It reveals all those elements of the self that need working on more directly than almost anything else. So don't be so stiff you cannot enjoy a joke with your colleagues. We are far more visible than we often imagine, yet we try to cultivate a front that hardly fools anybody. There is a huge relief that comes as we begin to let some of this go.

It is important to cultivate humility. By that I mean the keenness and willingness to learn and to be at peace with the fact that we do not know (when that is the case). Adequacy does not come from acquiring knowledge, or from acquiring anything for that matter. How much is enough? Those who crave certainty, love, recognition and respect are bound to feel they are inadequate, because however much they get they still need more. Yesterday's success is a nice memory, but then we need success again today. The same is true of reassurance and every other object of desire. These are all symptoms of not knowing the true nature. To know one's nature is not to know everything. When a person is grounded in their own nature, they can be humble without denigrating themselves.

In work, as in other areas of life, we can be driven by the feeling we don't quite measure up. Many people feel that they have a hole inside themselves, which can happen whenever we believe we are incomplete without something. It is common for people to think that their relationship with their parents was not adequate, that they were not loved sufficiently for themselves and they are now driven to fill this lack. This is spirituality driven by inadequacy, or the desire for what one lacks, rather than the exploration of what one has. You may have been deprived of love as a child, but you cannot go back. One must accept how it feels and give up blaming others or yourself for the situation and begin to see the treasures that are here right now. In time, you will come to see that you are complete along with the whole universe. Nothing in your past can prevent you from knowing the true nature now so long as you are willing to change.

Stress is quite a feature of life these days and not knowing one's true nature contributes to it. While it is good to see how stress can be reduced by changing the work environment and culture, one of the most important things is to come to recognize what really drives you.

Thinking Meditation

We have to come into the right relationship with our capacity to think. Thought itself is a wonderful attribute of the human mind, but we tend to overuse it, which is why these instructions contain so much about bringing it under control. Thought is not the enemy—we just need to learn how to use it. There are two levels to this. The first is what might be viewed as a common sense level. Here it helps to look at thinking in much the same way as you look at a physical task like cooking a meal. Focus yourself in the centre of it, decide what is the order of work and get on with it. If your thoughts wander to irrelevant matters, catch yourself and bring your thoughts back to the point. Listening to yourself is vital. Thoughts are mental objects passing through. Be aware of them and use them and recognize that to the thinker, thoughts are things. Your thoughts are not you, nor are they apart from you. When you listen to your thoughts, detect the point at which they start to drift, then bring yourself back by grounding yourself again. Maybe it's time to take a break and have a stretch. When I am writing, I find I waste a lot of time if I don't stop regularly. As your mindfulness develops, you should find your thinking becomes clearer and more focussed. It is unrestrained thought running you where it will that is the problem. As zazen deepens we come to a level where thought and zazen are one. This is thought as an activity and expression of the pure mind. However, without realization of the true nature this cannot be properly understood and it can only be learned in practice. Thought as an expression of true nature will manifest naturally as practice deepens, but this is another area where contact with a teacher is invaluable.

A dimension that should be brought in here, though, is our capacity to discern much more about a situation by *not* thinking than we can by thinking. I am referring to the open state of mind of zazen that is simply receptive within the heart of a situation.

The Utility of Not Knowing

Thinking is a reprocessing of information. Logic is useful in detecting inconsistency and falsehood, but it can only deal with the data it has. With zazen one is leaving behind knowing anything. This is quite different to the state of ignorance. The mind of zazen is to be open to what is, receptive and willing to see whatever may come however it may present itself. When we have a difficult choice, it is very important to just listen to the situation—its nuances, vibrations and general feel. This shows us the afflictions that may be active, as well as the aspects of compassion and wisdom that are there.

When viewing two possible options and trying to discern which is the right one, I need to be willing to do either and willing not to do either. The offering of that willingness allows some clarity. It may bring me face to face with my unwillingness to let go and if I see that, then I know the best thing is to stay with it. If I sit in the middle of the sense of unwillingness to give, the unwillingness will dissolve and then I can often see what to do. When someone in the monastery is acting disruptively, I need to be willing to continue to tolerate the situation and I need to be willing to ask them to leave. If I am unwilling to go down one of these roads, then my unwillingness affects my ability to see what is good. It is also important for me to know that there are often alternatives other than those that my limited imagination has presented me with so far.

One of the standard pieces of advice in counselling is not to be the expert who has a collection of fixes ready to hand out for every problem. Instead, listen to the person with an open heart and a deep compassionate acceptance. Don't impose your views or standards. Listen to and hear the person, because they will usually be able to discover the way forward themselves if given the room. We can apply the same principle to our own problems. The problem itself can be like the client in counselling—it contains its own solution if we are willing to be empty enough to receive it. There is never a solution that makes all the difficulties go away, yet we can see the next step that we need to take. Often that is not to do anything right now other than to be patient.

Listening Meditation

Listening is a vital ability when interacting with others; it parallels our ability to be still and hear ourselves. When people come for retreats at the monastery, they are often asked to help in the kitchen during work periods. The cook will sometimes give them a very specific task and show how he would like it done. Quite a few people find it difficult to hear and then follow the direction without having to raise a question or suggest how it might be done better, or they are just preoccupied with their suffering. In zazen it is not that there is some thing to be heard, like the cook's directions; to "hear" in zazen is to be sensitive to the pure mind and discern what is good to do, just as in practical situations one needs to hear the direction that is offered. Are we willing to serve or must we be the one in charge before anything can be done?

Quite often listening is difficult because it involves being with pain, either our own or someone else's. In Buddhism there are personifications of the attributes of enlightenment known as the Great Bodhisattvas. These include Manjusri, who represents wisdom, and Avalokiteshwara, who represents compassion. She is also known as Kanzeon in Japan and Kwan Yin in China and is the most popular of the Bodhisattvas. She is not a god or divinity, even though treated that way by some. To me, Kanzeon shows the compassionate nature of the universe. That each problem contains its own solution is an aspect of Kanzeon. She appears in any form in order to show beings the meaning of compassion. Kanzeon is the monastery cook, our mother, the official who seems obstructive and the aggressive beggar, but it takes a certain eye to see her in these guises. Her speciality is listening and one of her names translates as "She Who Hears the Cries of the World". What enables her to listen to all that agony without being destroyed herself is the ability to see the true nature of suffering. She can see beyond clinging, doubt, fear and despair to the true nature of life itself and of each being, knowing that she can absorb all the pain and let it dissolve. Although Kanzeon absorbs our pain if we call upon her, that will only be a temporary relief until we find her compassionate heart in ourselves. This is to find our true nature.

Learning zazen is learning to let our suffering arise and pass. In doing so, we can see it in a way that is impossible while we are driven by it. Kanzeon is not driven by the pain she hears, either into running away or into despair. She remains within her true nature, which is her compassionate heart, and has no shortage of strength. As humans we get exhausted, but even the exhausted mind retains its compassionate nature. Sometimes we may express the compassionate mind by resting when we can and by the willingness to go again whenever the call comes.

The more we learn how to sit still, the more we are able to hear, because we no longer need to avoid or fear suffering. This kind of freedom comes gradually as we train. Kanzeon just hears and in the quality of her hearing we are given the answer we need. Thus she responds to every call. Often we cannot do anything when confronted with suffering and we find that difficult. That is because we feel we have to add something of "me" to the situation—Kanzeon adds nothing and yet her influence extends everywhere. Although there are feelings associated with compassion, compassion is not a feeling. It is activity springing from the mind of zazen.

Political and Social Action

As citizens we have responsibilities to vote, to be informed to a degree and to recognize that the perpetration of evil is possible within a country when the population ignores it and does not respond to its arising. As part of our community, we have a duty to work for the good of others. Some may find their role in the field of politics. Politicians are easy targets for our cynicism. Personally, I am grateful that there are people willing to take on such a difficult job. As humans, their fears and desires get involved just as our own do. We should not be surprised that there is some self-serving. If we have none, then we might expect our politicians to have none. We should hold them to account, but refrain from simply being scornful. It is a myth that politicians are only in the job for what they can get. We should recognize the real wish to serve, even when there may be other elements also.

To get something done in this world takes a great deal of effort. To raise funds, to convince people to join an enterprise, to deal with all the regulations and endless details all takes great endurance. To be willing not only to ride the wagon, but to sometimes get out and push is a huge gift to the world. Those who make such an offering should be valued.

Buddhism advocates non-violence but is not pacifist—at least in my view, although others may disagree. What is clear, though, is that all volitional acts have consequences and those consequences are unavoidable. Not doing is also a volitional act. Buddhism, and zen in particular, does not get involved in detailed prescriptions of what is right and what is wrong, as that must be discerned in each situation. What is right is what is free of afflicted mental states, *i.e.* no greed, no anger and no delusion. It is up to us to cleanse our minds as best we are able and to act according to the needs of the situation, knowing that we are completely responsible for our actions.

The Monastic Life

In the Serene Reflection Meditation tradition, we value both the monastic and lay forms of training. The question arises for a lot of people as to whether they must be a monk to completely do this training. It is important to not let this question become a distraction. My advice is to discover how to do the meditation itself and how to keep going deeper through the willingness to change. Out of that practice will come the right means through which you can deepen your training. It is easy to confuse the imperative we feel to go deeper in training with becoming a monk, but these two are not necessarily the same. The percentage of people who enter a monastery is very small compared to the numbers who do this practice in the world of family, career and the so-called normal life. No life is normal; everyone has their own particular karmic tendencies to convert and each of us is ultimately responsible for choosing our way. The monastic way of life is the right medicine for some, but by no means for all, and if it is applied wrongly it can even cause harm. We each have to discern what the work is that comes to us for this life. It is not about our preferences but about how best we can give, bearing in mind our particular talents and needs. A theme I return to again and again is to just do the work that comes to you. Such an attitude is open-ended in the way that life itself is open. If you give yourself to the way, the way appears and that way is always changing.

CHAPTER 6

Skilful Means
in Zazen

"No method is easy and in the end
it is not a matter of perfecting a technique.
How do you sit still? Just sit still!"

ESPECIALLY IN THE beginning, zazen can feel very confusing. There seems to be no handle by which we can grasp it. The best advice is to keep going, as in a very direct way you are dealing with some of the fundamental problems that have to be overcome to realize your true nature. We have to entrust ourselves to the primordial pure mind of zazen rather than continually seeking reassurances and explanations, for ultimately there are none. In the end, there can be no mediation between you and zazen. Even though you may be sitting there wondering what on earth you are supposed to be doing, just treat that thought like any other thought and let it pass by. Ground yourself again and again and keep going. It is like learning to paint a picture—you have to splash some paint about and make a bit of a mess, but then gradually you get the feel of it as your faculties develop.

In the Serene Reflection Meditation tradition, we teach the basics of zazen at the beginning, rather than starting people off with a separate preliminary practice. We do this because there are no "methods" or means for doing zazen. Zazen is the fundamental primordial mind itself and the zen way of training and realization is to entrust oneself to it completely. It simply is; to approach it by any method is to add something to it and as soon as you attempt to do that, you have missed the point. In so doing, you believe that you stand outside seeking the doorway, when you are already "inside". To concern oneself with methods is not to trust the pure mind of zazen, a state Dōgen describes as the "dropping off of body and mind". The essential point of zazen is also lost, if one goes searching for the technique that is fastest, quickest, highest or whatever, for no technique can ever be zazen. I believe this point is important to understand at the outset so that one will use skilful means with discrimination and not let them obscure the real nature of zazen.

Yet within the Zen tradition, masters (including sometimes Dōgen himself) have always used skilful means to help awaken us to this fundamental mind. One of my favourite quotes attributed to Koho Zenji[1] is, "The truth, the whole truth and anything else that works!" We all need a helping hand to get started, and as training unfolds we should not be too idealistic or too proud to accept help. My advice is to use skilful means when you need them and seek the advice of a teacher who can help you

[1] Keidō Chisan Kohō Zenji was Rev. Master Jiyu's master, and Abbot of Sōjiji, one of the main temples of the Sōtō School in Japan.

find the heart of zazen directly. As soon as the means have achieved their purpose, then return to the effort to do pure zazen and "just sit".

Circular Breathing

This method was recommended by Rev. Master Jiyu. It is an imaginative exercise to begin with in which you picture your breath as starting at the base of your spine, then as you breathe in you picture the breath as rising up your spine to the top of your head. As you breathe out, picture the breath moving down the centre line of your front to the pubic bone so that the "breath" forms a circle. Breathing in, up the back, breathing out, down the front. Keep this going for three or four breaths to start yourself off when beginning a period of zazen or when you find yourself getting lost or distracted. Breathe normally when doing this, *i.e.* not especially deeply but just as it comes. This practice is not designed to be used all the time, but just as a means of focussing yourself. It links in with the basic movement of chi within zazen and can be of great help. It can be used in conjunction with the grounding practice.

What to Do When Falling Asleep or Sitting Like a Pudding

A common difficulty is falling into drowsiness—not actually falling asleep but going into a drifting semi-anaesthetized fog. Your posture slumps and you rock forward and then catch yourself with a start, but usually not enough of a jerk to actually wake you up! This state is familiar territory to anyone who tries to meditate for very long. The best advice is to check your posture, open your eyes wide for a moment and take a deep breath and carry on sitting. Sometimes, however, nothing seems to work and although you may not be really exhausted, you find yourself dozing off again. Keeping going when this happens is really doing something useful, even though it may not seem like it; if you give in to drowsiness, it will never pass.

Laxity of mind is a problem related to drowsiness, although it may not be quite so noticeable. Zazen can reveal uncomfortable feelings and somewhat unconsciously we opt for being only partly present. One can waste years of practice by not focussing on what you are doing. This is sitting like a pudding rather than like a mountain! You have to bring all of yourself to the party to meditate properly. It helps to ground yourself, as described in chapter two. If you still keep wandering in a dreamy way, then it may help to count your breaths as detailed below. Please remember, though, that the technique itself won't do it; you have to use the technique to focus your mind and really be present. If you do that, you can cure "pudding mind" right away.

Counting Your Breaths

This is a concentration exercise that can be used now and again to help you focus your mind, but it is best not to let it become your main practice. To try this, keep your mind on the rise and fall of your abdomen as you breathe in and out and then count each out-breath. By developing a strong focus on this deliberate foreground of meditation, you exclude thoughts by concentrating on the breath count. You may notice thoughts passing through in the background and that is no problem, as long as you do not lose your place in the count. Count your out-breaths up to ten and then start again. If you lose your place in the count, then without giving rise to irritation, quietly go back to the beginning again. You may find it quite difficult to actually make it to ten. Don't worry about it, just keep going. After doing this for some time, a feeling of concentration begins to develop if you keep at it. There is also a degree of peacefulness that comes at the same time, because you are no longer scattered and are much more in control of yourself. Familiarize yourself with this feeling of being centred, it is a helpful bench mark, then go back to just sitting in zazen. It is useful to count your breaths for a meditation period every now and again just as a diagnostic test for pudding mind! It can be a bit of a salutary shock! However, pudding mind can and does come and go in a moment. If you find you are caught up in a dreamy state, it is just another mental affliction to let go of.

It is easy to underestimate how long it takes to get the feel of zazen and to start casting about for alternatives; don't jump the gun and start counting the breaths when you may not need to. Regular contact with a teacher can help in this area. There are many other devices like these that a skilled teacher can show you when they are called for, but over the last thirty years I have been impressed with people's natural ability to find their way into the practice if they keep going. No method is easy and in the end it is not a matter of perfecting a technique. How do you sit still? Just sit still! Everyone finds it difficult to start with so do not underestimate your capacity.

CHAPTER 7

Some Mistakes
to Avoid

*"We have to be willing to fall apart...in the sense that we
let go of all our self-images and come to a real spiritual poverty.
It is in such a place that the true nature is found."*

PEOPLE OFTEN HAVE the idea that zazen is about experiencing blissful states and if they do not experience such things, they think that either
they are doing something wrong or else zazen doesn't work. Blissful states
do arise from time to time, but they are not enlightenment. This is because
they are fleeting and when one emerges from them, the three poisons of
greed, hatred and delusion can still arise again, as one has not yet cut their
root. Mind you, there is nothing wrong with these states and they can be
of enormous help in confirming that there are fruits to be experienced on
the way—and all too easily we make them into another object of desire
and find that our minds grasp after them.

If all the Buddhas come to greet you or all the devils come to pursue
you—either way—the path of zazen is to sit still, not chasing after the

one or fleeing the other. The true nature is beyond all appearances. We may "see" all kinds of things with the mind's eye; all such images are just images that appear, we should not hold on to them or push them away. Just treat them like another thought. They may contain good teaching or they may contain delusive teaching. If we do not hanker after them, time will put them into their proper perspective. We so much want confirmation that we can inadvertently make such things the object of our practice and that is a mistake.

To free ourselves from delusion involves seeing the nature of the delusions we are subject to. This is sometimes painful, yet to be able to see them is a real mark of progress. This means that if we try to assess our meditation according to whether it is pleasant or unpleasant, then we are likely to misjudge it.

People can sometimes approach zen like a customer in a supermarket buying a product that should fix their suffering. Unfortunately, sometimes this attitude is fostered by the way spiritual traditions try to sell themselves. Training is not a contract in which you can buy certain benefits. Often we can get caught in looking for the fix, the magic that will do it for us, whether we conceive it as a technique or a revelation. All these pitfalls miss the essential point: training is not about boosting the self; it is about letting the self fall away. Those who are very competent in their career and have a lot of valuable skills can come to the practice seeking to become an expert, just as they have successfully done in other areas of life. This will not work with meditation, although sometimes the appearance that is created can be deceptive. The "I" can seek an appearance of spiritual competence in which it can hide by imitating the true nature. We have to be willing to fall apart, not in the sense of a psychological disintegration, but in the sense that we let go of all our self-images and come to a real spiritual poverty. It is in such a place that the true nature is found.

It is possible to try too hard in meditation. The effort needed is to bring oneself to sit and to patiently and quietly accept what comes and let it flow on. If we are trying to make things happen, to force our way in, then, again, we obstruct ourselves. We have to do our part and let go and trust the true nature. Many people find that their practice oscillates between trying very hard and then giving up. Suffering brings them to training, then with practise the suffering eases a bit and so they stop before the root of the suffering has been truly seen. Regularity of meditation is a great help with this, especially if we let go of trying to assess our practice.

Although there are many mistakes, it is still necessary to trust that you are doing it right unless something shows you that you are not—in which case just take that on board and alter course accordingly. It may be that we each have to make our own mistakes along the path as part of the learning process, so we should not fear mistakes or we can paralyze ourselves. At the same time, it makes sense to seek help from those with enough experience to be able to help us see more clearly. A good teacher will not judge or condemn; in all likelihood, they will be able to spot the mistake because they have made it themselves.

If we should realize that we have made a mistake, one that perhaps has caused suffering to others, then it is important to acknowledge it and do what you can to put it right, but not to beat oneself up about it. All the great masters of the past have made their share of mistakes, some of them very serious indeed, yet they still went on to true realization and were able to be of great help to others. We cannot go back, but we can learn and accept the consequences of what we have done without complaint. Some of the simplest and best advice I have ever been given in the spiritual life is never give up.

CHAPTER 8

Morality, the Precepts and Zen

*"To realize Buddha Nature is to know
that nothing is missing and within that completeness
there is great compassion for all beings."*

ZEN TEACHES THAT all beings are the Buddha Nature. Buddha Nature is the unmediated state of how things really are, the true nature of reality. It is called Buddha Nature because it is the essence of the Buddha's enlightenment. Nobody possesses Buddha Nature; because there is nothing that is outside of it to possess, its nature is non-duality and includes everything. To realize Buddha Nature is to know that nothing is missing and within that completeness there is great compassion for all beings. This great compassion is not merely a feeling. It is an essential aspect of Buddha Nature; it is part of how things are and is fundamental to existence. When we realize our true nature, we realize compassion and that compassion manifests as the wish to help all beings. To realize this wish is to know the true purpose of life and then the practical questions of how to live are no longer addressed from the point of view of "What do I want?", but from the perspective of "What is it that is good to do?" "Good" is that which helps beings; it is something we have an intuitive knowledge of when we entrust ourselves to the Buddha Nature. Each person has to discover how to manifest compassion in his or her life—the principles are the same for everyone, but the specifics will depend upon each person's circumstances and abilities. No progress can be made unless one is willing to let go of selfish desires. It is important that we have faith in the purity of our essential being, as we shall need to trust ourselves both in order to meditate deeply and to discern the good.

Although we have a fundamental nature that is pure, we get caught up in the three poisons—greed, anger and delusion. Once we really see the three poisons for what they are, the motivation to be free of them is present. We are sometimes half-hearted in our efforts to clean up our minds, because we do not let ourselves see what we are doing. For instance, to actually see anger or hatred in oneself in all its nakedness, without excusing it, and indeed without deflecting it by condemning ourselves, is to *know* we do not wish to give rise to it ever again. Such initial realization changes how we act, but we may still sometimes get angry despite our best intentions. There is an end to delusion, but it takes endless training to realize it. Those who truly practise zazen do not see themselves as enlightened nor do they see themselves as unenlightened; they quietly do that which needs to be done, looking for no reward. Such people find themselves in the midst of enlightenment. In order to come to this place, we need a deep commitment to training. That commitment lies within the pure mind of zazen and it must also be acted upon in the world; our actions will demonstrate our understanding of it.

People are sometimes repelled by the word morality, because it conjures up images of having to follow an inflexible set of arbitrary or meaningless rules that are enforced by a hypocritical authority. Morality is not about condemning others; it is not bigotry, nor is it something dreamed up by ruling elites to keep us in our place. Morality is not about authority, either a divine authority who threatens us with punishment, nor a human authority who takes it upon themselves to decide what others should do. Morality comes out of our natural wish to do good. Our sense of good may be rather small-scale and restricted just to ourselves and those close to us, or it may be more universal in character, but we all believe that there are virtues that are admirable and actions that are wrong. Many would uphold the "Golden Rule" of do as you would have others do to you. Morality is based upon sympathy, which is the recognition that others feel happiness and pain just as we do. Our wants and desires are in conflict with those of others as long as we are acting selfishly, *i.e.* believing we are separate from the rest. Such belief carries the price of separation from our true nature and any chance of being at peace.

Buddhism offers a means to help us clarify for ourselves what is good and what is not in the form of the Precepts. When we act in accord with our true nature, then we keep the Precepts. The formulation of the Precepts serves as a skilful means to help us discern what is good. They are also a description of the true nature in action. They can be used as a checklist when considering what is good. Much more than that, the Precepts are one with Buddhahood itself. Being and action are not divided— what we do and what we are cannot be separated. A Buddha is not limited by the Precepts, because the Precepts and his or her true nature are exactly the same. The Precepts are regarded as the great liberators, as they point the way and help us avoid suffering.

If we do not act well, then we feel shame. By acknowledging our shame, we can rectify our life. The motive to rectify our wrong actions comes when we see how they separate us from what is most valuable and true. If we discover that we are doing something that is not good, then straight away we need to change course. There is no need for self-condemnation or guilt. This is easier said than done, of course. All our defensiveness can rise up and we may try to justify what we really know to be a mistake so as not to feel we have been wrong. One of the first things one learns about zazen is that it is necessary to be willing to feel foolish. If we are willing to recognize a mistake and accept whatever feelings come with that realization, then we are already wise.

There are sixteen Precepts in the Sōtō Zen tradition of Dōgen.

The Three Refuges

I take refuge in the Buddha;
I take refuge in the Dharma;
I take refuge in the Sangha.

The Three Pure Precepts

Cease from evil;
Do only good;
Do good for others.

The Ten Precepts

These are expressed in the form, "Do not…" kill, etc. The use of "do not" is not indicating an authority, divine or otherwise, who imposes these Precepts. The voice of "do not" is our own; the imperative comes from knowing the infinitely compassionate nature of the true mind.

Do not kill.

Do not steal.

Do not covet.

Do not say that which is untrue.

Do not sell the wine of delusion.

Do not speak against others.

Do not be proud of yourself and devalue others.

Do not be mean in giving either Dharma or wealth.

Do not be angry.

Do not defame the Three Treasures.

The Precepts are taken as a commitment and that is how one formally becomes a Buddhist. It is necessary to commit ourselves to act in accord with our true nature. Our integrity as a Buddhist depends upon it. The Three Refuges come first as the fundamental commitments of a Buddhist. We take refuge in the Buddha as a teacher, having some faith in his teaching and the integrity of his life. He is not seen as divine but as the great exemplar. The Buddha refuge also includes those who are our teachers and who exemplify the teaching for us. Because our true nature is Buddha Nature, we need also to respect our own existence as Buddha. That means having faith and trust in oneself. One is far more likely to act well, if one has such self-respect. Refuge in the Dharma is to be open to the Buddha's teaching in the sūtras and the teaching we receive through our experience of life—for all things teach when we have an open heart. To take refuge in the Sangha is to recognize the natural authority of those who have been in training longer than we have, or whose understanding is deeper than our own, and to seek advice and counsel from them. The term *Sangha* is traditionally applied to ordained men and women who have left home, live a celibate life and devote their lives to training and helping others. However, one's fellow lay trainees can be an excellent source of help and encouragement too. In the widest meaning of the term, Sangha includes all who follow the Buddha's way. Some show how to train by example, others by showing what not to do. It takes both courage and humility to take refuge in the Three Treasures.

Cease from evil, the first of the Three Pure Precepts, is the source of right action. When we cease from evil, we leave room for our fundamental purity to shine of itself. Once we recognize that our true wish is to do only good, the second of the Three Pure Precepts, we need to commit ourselves to that good. It is not enough to pay lip service to the idea of the good—it must become the centre of our lives. Our commitment helps us to keep going through the lifelong process of training. Old habits are hard to break and a lot of work has to be done to put aside delusions as they arise. This is possible when we allow ourselves to be centred enough, or still enough, to recognize what is happening. The guide is our intuitive sense of sympathy and compassion; for example, is it good to take this object that I desire? If I am committed to doing only good, then all that matters is what is good to do. My desires are no longer primary and that is the key feature of committing oneself to doing only good. Desires are simply desires; it is how we respond to them that matters. Therefore, any thoughts, feelings or emotions can be allowed to arise within zazen without the need to judge them. However, we need to recognize that there is a line between naturally-occurring thoughts and following those thoughts. A memory may arise of how someone has hurt a person whom I love and I find that I am angry. To cease from evil is to not feed that anger. This means bringing to an end the rehashing of the incident over and over in my mind. To do only good is to determine to sit within the anger without suppressing or indulging it.

The Precepts are not intended to be taken as absolutes to be followed in all circumstances without regard for the consequences. Where there are conflicts between the Ten Precepts, one takes the question to the level of the Three Pure Precepts. Cease from evil contains all the other Precepts. Do only good is the personal commitment, whereas do good for others is the Bodhisattva vow to save all beings before one has saved oneself; it implies the necessity to act for the benefit of others and is a positive injunction.

The Precepts begin with having enough faith in oneself to be prepared to look honestly at our intentions and our actions. If we are going against any of the Precepts, we need to be particularly careful of what we are doing. We are responsible for our actions and will receive the consequences that flow from them. My teacher always used to say, "Zen is a religion for spiritual adults". Sometimes there are conflicting needs and it is hard to see what is right. Zazen helps in these situations. There is no absolute rule we can apply; we can only do the very best we can for all beings. The Precepts do not give us a free run, in the sense that if we keep them we do not have to think about what we do. Doing that which is good cannot be done by any formula. Committing ourselves to the Precepts commits us in the realm of action. What we do with intent has real consequence; it has effects that condition the present and future state of our minds for good or ill. Intellectual views are important, they can help us move in the right direction, but in the final analysis, it is what we do that matters. We cannot keep the Precepts by just reining ourselves in—

they are there to guide and encourage our going forward. To do nothing out of fear of making a mistake is the saddest mistake.

Each year at the larger monasteries of the Order there is a week-long retreat called *Jukai* especially for receiving the Precepts. The week includes a series of special ceremonies that act out the meaning of the Precepts in profound and moving ways. It is the most popular retreat of the year. By formally receiving the Precepts, one affirms something very deep within oneself and so this week is often a turning-point in people's lives.

CHAPTER 9

Gratitude

"To awaken the desire for enlightenment is crucial.
There can be no little corners left outside of that desire,
although it takes everyone time and a lot of effort
to offer up all their hiding places. This is just when the
gratitude really sings..."

ONE OF THE SIGNS of enlightenment is gratitude. It is the song of the heart in response to the Buddha Nature. The more one trusts the Buddha Nature and lives by its prompting, the more gratitude there is. Sometimes gratitude is felt deeply and it fills everything; at other times one may not consciously be aware of it. If one's life is rooted in the Buddha Nature, then it is never far away, even when training feels like wading through syrup. It is a confirmation that one is not totally off the path, but it is unwise to take it as confirmation of any particular feature of training. Gratitude does not judge: even while one is still seeing the world from the point of view of a self, there can be gratitude; when one lets go of the self, gratitude is unlimited and the heart overflows.

Gratitude is an innate aspect of Buddha Nature and it is good to cultivate it. By doing so, we come closer to the Buddha Nature. Cultivation uncovers the gratitude that is already present rather than creating it. The means of cultivating gratitude are many, but they all begin with respect.

Buddhists in Japan use the gasshō, also known as *anjali* or *namasté*, where the palms and fingers are placed together in a gesture of respect or reverence. As well as expressing gratitude, it is used as a greeting since one wishes to respect others. If one is not feeling gratitude and respect at the time, then the gesture is used to express one's aspiration to find these qualities. When entering the Buddha hall one always makes gasshō and bows. During the ceremonies performed each morning, everyone makes full prostrations to the Buddha and to each other. These are not means one can necessarily use outside the monastery, but the mind that is expressed in these gestures can be expressed in many other forms. To ask, "How are you doing?" can be just a commonplace or a real expression of concern.

New monks receive a lot of correction. Every detail of their behaviour that is not mindful, or does not express the commitment of a monk, is liable to be pointed out to them by a senior. After the third time in one morning, the gasshō that is made in acknowledgement can get a little stiff, but "mumphing" is not permitted! One has to let go of the irritation. We all encounter trying situations, the more so when feeling tense and under pressure. While we may forgive ourselves for swearing and lapsing into justification, that does nothing for our training. "Sympathy is as the sea, in that all waters may gather and form only one sea."[1] The sea is the Buddha Nature. The cost of enlightenment sometimes seems high—until

[1] *Shushōgi*, Great Master Dōgen, translated by Rev. Master Jiyu-Kennett in *Zen Is Eternal Life*, 4th ed. (Mt. Shasta, CA: Shasta Abbey Press, 1999).

one enters the sea. The novice may not succeed every time in responding with respect, but they should be in no doubt about what it takes to enter the sea.

Anger works against gratitude and respect. The Buddhist attitude towards anger is to see it as an affliction, since it clouds the mind and prevents us from seeing clearly. Mental states are assessed according to whether they are conducive to, or hinder, enlightenment. Anger is therefore seen as a poison. In Western culture, we have the idea of a justifiable anger, or moral outrage, which is seen as a good thing as it can motivate us in response to injustice. The motivation in Buddhism comes from compassion. Compassion can be fierce when it has to be, but it is never mixed with anger; if it is, then it is an afflicted state of mind and not compassion. If there is a right motivation arising within us in response to injustice, then it is not anger. From the Buddhist perspective, there is no justification for anger, although one should have great sympathy for oneself and for others when there has been great suffering or injustice inflicted. Anger in the end will not help, although one may have to go through a time of uncovering anger that has been suppressed. A response to injustice is much less likely to cause further injustice, if it is based not on anger but compassion. Buddhists, like most people, get angry but they view their anger as something they need to let go of. From such a perspective, whatever happens in life can be taken as part of one's training. Then there are no real barriers because one's path cannot be blocked—yet there is some pretty difficult training.

If one can see that whatever happens is a means of training, then one can approach it with gratitude. To begin with while one is finding the path, just like the novice, one's gasshō may be tense and a lot of *sotto voce*

swearing may go on underneath; yet if one's intention is for enlightenment, then training is possible. To awaken the desire for enlightenment is
crucial. There can be no little corners left outside of that desire, although
it takes everyone time and a lot of effort to offer up all their hiding places.
This is just when the gratitude really sings, because it is the moment one
discovers the great treasure of the Buddha Nature.

It is of great benefit to offer the merit of one's efforts in training to
the good of all beings, to cultivate gratitude to the Buddha for the teaching and to recognize how much one is given in this life. Every day to
devote one's life to the good of all beings releases one from a great deal of
suffering. One then receives so much merit that there is so much more to
give. Merit in Buddhism is seen as those good qualities and benefits that
accrue through training and right action. The way of the Bodhisattva is
to dedicate all that merit to others so that they may realize the truth. It is
a means of offering loving-kindness, especially to those in difficult situations for whom one can do little or nothing in a practical way.

CHAPTER 10

Zazen in Its Religious Context

*"Our purpose is to realize enlightenment,
which includes discovering the true nature
of oneself and all of existence."*

TODAY, MEDITATION IS increasingly taught in a non-religious context, for example as the practice of mindfulness to help sufferers from depression and a host of other difficulties. I feel much benefit can be derived from this kind of approach, and it is good to see some of the benefits of Buddhist practice being made available to people who might not otherwise find them. The therapeutic uses of meditation aim towards developing a relative normality, a less-disturbed state and a greater degree of acceptance, whereas the fundamental aim of Buddhist practice goes much further. Our purpose is to realize enlightenment, which includes discovering the true nature of oneself and all of existence. This involves letting go of all greed, hatred and delusion so that there are no obstructions to the opening of the heart of compassion and wisdom. I see these two aims, the therapeutic and that of enlightenment, as part of one continuum; but if one's wish is to realize enlightenment, then one has to go far beyond the therapeutic context. Buddhism points to the potential of enlightenment, which we can realize if we are prepared to go far enough.

Zazen is at the heart of this process, yet if one only ever sits in meditation, there are aspects of enlightenment that one can quite possibly never realize. It is not that zazen itself is a limited practice, rather it is that if we *only* do sitting zazen, then we place a limitation on that which goes far beyond any one form. Enlightenment includes the kaleidoscopic mind that is able to see the truth in everything.

When visiting the monastery, people are sometimes surprised to see the ceremonies that take place each day, the occasional festivals and other religious forms that we have. In the last chapter, I described how bowing is part of our practice and I well remember my first visit to the monastery and how self-conscious I felt about this. Because people are often drawn to Buddhism due to its rational basis and lack of insistence on dogma or belief, they find ceremonies and religious forms harder to relate to than the basic practice of meditation. But these religious or devotional dimensions have a great value and form an important part of our tradition. Their very unfamiliarity can take us to places in ourselves that we might otherwise miss. Ceremonies are a means of expressing gratitude and by giving it expression, we come to know it more deeply. To attend a ceremony as an observer will not be much help to us, whereas to take part with an open heart allows one to feel from the inside what it is about. When I stopped worrying about being self-conscious and just bowed, something inside connected with the physical action and it became a real expression of something deep within me that I might not have otherwise known. This is a kind of knowing that is different to that of the intellect; it is far more visceral and direct.

Each morning the whole community comes together and sings the scriptures that are at the heart of the teaching. After a surprisingly short time, one begins to memorize them and they are thus always available. The scriptures are extremely distilled and at first only some of the meaning is clear, but as one's training deepens they have greater and greater meaning and sometimes seem to be pointing the way.

It is common for Buddhists to have an altar somewhere in their home. It usually consists of a small statue of the Buddha with a candle, some flowers, a water offering and an incense bowl. It is helpful to offer some incense or just light the candle before sitting and make three bows towards the altar. To what is one bowing? For myself I find it best not to form a conception, and I certainly do not wish to bow to any *conception*. Like the primordial mind of zazen, one does not need to add anything or take anything away. To just bow, to just be present, opens up a profound depth within that is best left to 'speak' for itself. The altar represents but does not define it. It reminds me of what is important and becomes a focus through which I can reorient myself when confronting confusion and doubt, and it also serves as a focus when I wish to give expression to my deepest intention in training. For me, therefore, an altar does not imply a god, rather it points to the infinite depth of this moment.

CHAPTER II

Death

*"Dōgen advises us not to seek a Buddha outside
of birth and death. This means not searching for an absolute
that is somehow beyond birth and death."*

TO FIND FREEDOM in this life, one has to come to terms with death
and the suffering of dying. We have to contemplate the end of our existence as we know it and our fears that surround this question. The Buddha pointed to what he considered to be two wrong views: that death is
a complete cessation of life; and that the self is, in some form, immortal.
To face death is to face the unknown. People are all too willing to come
up with great certainties, but for me, even if they do *know*, I do not, and
their telling me will still remain their certainty and not my own. Whether
beliefs are true or not is not the point, if for oneself they are just a belief.
No concepts about the nature of life and death will bring liberation.

This leaves only the one thing we have had all along—the unmediated life and death of this moment. To add anything is unnecessary and
will only obscure the completeness of it. One must trust oneself utterly
to this moment and be content with the life that is now. In accepting life
and death in this way, we let go of everything that we think and believe

and love and hate—everything. Then in this moment, there is no concern about death. This is not simply putting the thought of death out of one's mind; it is going into the heart of what we fear death to be—the end of all we hold on to. When you stop holding on, even now while still alive, you know that all is well, yet that is knowing nothing. If you try and carry the knowledge with you, it becomes more baggage that obscures the moment. Whenever we discover such baggage, it is best to offer it up into the infinity of the present moment. The sufficiency of this moment cannot be described; it is empty of everything, even of emptiness itself.

This approach takes the courage to seek what is and not just count in the treasury of others. To understand this approach we need to see that zazen is not a means to an end; it is life right now. When you sit, you are one with original enlightenment; when you die, you are one with original enlightenment—just don't obscure it.

Buddhism uses all kinds of skilful means to talk about how karmic consequence works, how actions in this life affect future lives and how our present life is the result of past lives. The wheel of life is used as an analogy for the way in which deluded action leads to more delusion in an endless cycle while we remain ignorant of the true mind. These teachings are vitally important, but we still need something more: the realization for ourselves of the truth of this moment. We do not need to experience past lives in order to know this. If we chase after knowing our past lives, then we become like the man shot with an arrow in the parable told by the Buddha. The man refused to let the arrow be taken out until he knew who shot it, what caste he was from, why he shot it and so on, so that in the end the man needlessly died. To take the arrow out is to let go of delusion right now. If I see a tendency to be angry, I still have to let that anger dissolve in the moment of its arising. Once I do that there is no anger. I do not then become a person with no anger; there is nothing to carry away. Experience in this life and in past lives may show us the terrible cost of not letting our anger go, but the step into actualizing "cease from evil" is only now.

We should not think of ourselves as a septic tank full of horrible delusion that has to be removed. We are empty from the beginning, yet we are capable of manifesting delusion right now. Part of that delusion is to believe one is a septic tank full of filth. We should not think we are pure either. When I use the expression the "pure mind", this is pure in the sense of empty, there being nothing to hold on to outside this present moment. There is no real person who is either pure or impure. However, without genuine realization and training we cannot know this purity and when we do not know it, we get caught up all the more in delusion. When it is time to die, we can go forward in the mind of zazen, bringing neither purity nor impurity with us.

Most people fear the process of dying more than death. As we gain experience of zazen, we see how it is possible to endure and how, in fact, we do endure. In a very simple way, when you come to a week retreat, some of the sitting periods seem to go on forever. If you sit and complain or fuss and constantly try and look at your watch, then it seems almost unendurable. We can learn how much we are the creators of our own suffering. In a retreat, usually about the fourth day, most people give up worrying about their discomfort and find there is an energy that carries them through. It still takes effort, but a lot of the resistance has evaporated. The same principle works when we suffer illness. It is not the same, and yet just as we don't have to run away in the retreat, so we don't have to run away from our illness. It is the training that comes to us; it is our life. If we know how to do zazen, then we find the moment has all we need. There is nothing wrong in accepting pain killers—they may be the appropriate "food" for that time. Yes, it may be hard, but what makes it hard are the things we still have to let go of, so here is the opportunity.

The Sōtō tradition has a beautiful funeral ceremony designed to point the way to the immaculate nature. The body is placed upon the altar because it, too, is Buddha. The coffin is usually open at the beginning of the ceremony so people can say their farewells and so that the process of dying is not hidden. It is the mind with which the ceremony is done that matters most; this depends on the priest and everyone together. Even those who know nothing of Buddhism and the forms that are used can take part and find it helpful. Life does not end, nor is there a beginning. Often people have beliefs that are comforting. Our way is not to destroy those beliefs, as they can work to bring people to the truth. Death shows how little time we have. There is no need for sectarianism, especially around death where all such things seem petty and foolish. One of the great features of Buddhism is the understanding that the truth does not have to insist upon itself.

The problem of death is inseparable from the problem of life. Dōgen advises us not to seek a Buddha outside of birth and death. This means not searching for an absolute that is somehow beyond birth and death. The Buddha refuge is this moment or it is a fantasy, since there is nothing else. This is why Dōgen insists that zazen is the only gateway to the truth. He is not making a sectarian statement; he is pointing out that zazen and the present moment are inseparable. We can call it anything we like, but we should beware of adding anything to it. This is something that a lifetime of zazen helps us to see. When finally letting go, we can accept what we have resisted for so long—the utterly open heart.

CHAPTER 12

Buddha Bows to Buddha

"The first thing is always to bow.
This is the outer action of the inner intent
to let go of everything."

IT IS NOT AN easy thing to sit in zazen and face oneself. Yet we have a remarkable capacity for courage and perseverance, although sometimes it may not seem that way and it is easy to doubt and give up. The Buddha Nature calls to us and we know there is something more than chasing after fleeting satisfactions and achievements in this life. There is a yearning to realize the truth that lies within the heart of everyone. This yearning is life itself, the movement to grow and flourish to the fullness of our being. It can be trusted to show us the way, to know what is good to do, when we actually trust it in practice and follow it rather than just hold it as an ideal. Often people do not recognize this yearning for what it is and mistakenly chase after things in the world and turn this yearning into greed. This can be turned around, when one looks closely at what we are really seeking within greed. The trouble is we are not usually in the habit of looking rigorously enough and so we get lost in craving.

In an earlier chapter, I wrote of how our lives and our minds are inter-related with everything else, that the "I" has no separate existence. One of the joys that flows from this is our deep connection to all of life. It is because of this connectedness that we can know what is good to do. It does not make us infallible, since our ability to discern in any situation is subject to being obscured by our fear, desire or confusion, but at root that connection with all that is, is complete. Its totality is more than the sum of its parts; this is the miraculous nature of life.

For me, there is a deep aspect of devotion within the Buddhist life of training. To bow in gratitude each morning and evening is a joy and a way in which the heart can be kept open. To what does one bow? I find that devotion in itself is enough, to offer one's gratitude to the Buddha means to me to offer it to all the world—there is no Buddha outside of the world and no world outside of the Buddha. The Buddha statue that I bow towards represents the Buddha Mind that ultimately is inexpressible in any abstract terms, yet it can be known in the living of one's life. The more I am in touch with it, the more I can see it in the people and things around me. One day that statue looks rather tired and sad, another day it seems to smile with an infinite acceptance of me and all beings. Such changes are in my own mind. I note their reflections and try to live appropriately to the circumstances of the day. The first thing is always to bow. This is the outer action of the inner intent to let go of everything. When all is offered up, there is deep unobstructed freedom to do that which is good. It is foolish to believe that by giving we lose something, when the truth is the exact opposite. We should value those opportunities that come our way to give, whether materially or spiritually, as they are the means through which we grow in the life of training. We should not hesitate to give others the opportunity of giving also—it is good to ask for help, it is good to live connectedly.

I find it easy to get lost in the theory of Buddhism by trying to pin down what the Buddha is or is not. It is far more important to do zazen. One does need the framework of right views, and spending time studying the teaching is worthwhile, but a clear sense of its limitation is important. In the Zen tradition, we do not rely upon words and concepts as the means of realizing the truth. Our way is to point directly to the truth that is within all of us, to trust it and live from it with all the commitment we can muster. We don't have to make a picture of it, we don't have to make it into an object that is separate from us or above us in some way, yet it is far more than our egocentric self. We bow to what is greater and we bow to what is within and learn to give up making distinctions between them. When there are no distinctions, there is no self to hold on to; there is this great movement and flow of life itself: Buddha recognizes Buddha and Buddha bows to Buddha.